T0195707

EMBRACING THE SHIFT

Understanding The Different Stages
Of Process In Your Faith Walk

WAYMOND L. MCKISSICK

WESTBOW
P R E S S®
A DIVISION OF THOMAS NELSON
& ZONDERVAN

WestBow Press books may be ordered through booksellers or by contacting:

WestBow Press
A Division of Thomas Nelson & Zondervan
1663 Liberty Drive
Bloomington, IN 47403
www.westbowpress.com
1 (866) 928-1240

ISBN: 978-1-9736-8911-9 (sc)
ISBN: 978-1-9736-8910-2 (e)

Library of Congress Control Number: 2020905622

Print information available on the last page.

WestBow Press rev. date: 4/27/2020

FOREWORD

FROM THE TIME I HEARD of the birth of this book I knew God had prepared a message through and in the Life of Prophet Waymond L McKissick Sr that would bless the many lives that this publication would reach, of the many ones who long for God but have failed so many times. It's through His personal encounters that He has interwoven life's victories and setbacks that assure us that maintaining a lifestyle through Christ we are overcomers!

Prophet McKissick has been very transparent and I am sure that you will be blessed beyond measure as he quiescent us through the paths of rediscover Our Faith In Christ. I know that you will be blessed as you read each page to unlock God's good from within you!

(Philippians 1:6 Amplified Translation)
Bishop Derrick S Johnson Sr
Sr Pastor
New Creation Family Worship Center

INTRODUCTION

HAVE YOU EVER BEEN IN a place where everything around you is swirling around? When at first, everything was going your way. You had the best life ever. Then God needs you to come closer to Him. Then all of a sudden life throws you for a loop?

Hi, my name is Waymond Lee McKissick and I have been through the shift. This book was written to encourage someone that may be in the middle of a shift or getting ready to go into one.

I've been preaching since I was 6 years old. At the age of 12 I understood the gift over my life as a prophet. At the age of 27 I started my first church (Shekinah Christian Fellowship Church). I pastored there for 10 years before relinquishing my pastoral duties to the most trusted associate Pastors James and Michelle Stapleton Morris. Then in 2012 I started my 2nd church (Fresh Word Church).

Needless to say, through these journeys of life I have been through a lot of changes. However, going through a shift is something different from any change I have ever encountered in my life.

My prayer is that this book blesses someone that may be going through a shift right now. I wish I had listened better as different men of God were talking about their times of shift. I have been blessed to serve with some great men of God. Bishop Michael Thomas: whom I started under from the age of 6 until I was 26 years old. He taught me what it means to fight for your people. The first example of faith I saw. Then God sent Apostle Reginald White, who led me personally and gave me my prophetic confirmation.

He has been a great pastor to me and a great voice of God to me. The word of revelation that comes out of this man's mouth is mind blowing.

Another man that has been a great mentor to me is Apostle Darrel McCoy. He never says much but what he does say is very precious. These 3 men of God will always be in my heart. I have seen God work in their lives and how God has used them to help mold me. The thing is with all the changes they have helped me through. With all the development they have help me with. Nothing prepared me for this shift. A change is something you can identify in yourself and make the necessary adjustment. The Shift is what God identifies in you that only he can change. It may be something you can see but don't know how to change yourself. If you want to be and go to the next level, then you must go through next level training. THE SHIFT.

CONTENTS

ONE

EMBRACING THE SHIFT

HAVE YOU EVER STARTED A job from ground level and after being there for a week you got promoted to C.E.O? If your answer is yes, then I need that job.

However, for most of us the answer would be no. In most jobs you start from the bottom and work your way to the top. Every job has a process for promotion and advancement.

It's not that different with the kingdom of God. There are different levels that we all would love to get to.

You must know that there is a process to every level of anointing in the kingdom. Even though we were all born with a purpose. The bible says,

The Lord gave me this message 5. "I knew you before I formed you in your mother's womb. Before you were born, I set you apart and appointed you as my prophet to the nations." (Jeremiah 1:4-5 NLT)

This lets us know that even though you're purposed, there are still levels of maturity and process you must go through to get to where God wants you to be. We are all born with gifts and callings, however we don't all start out mature enough to handle those gifts; nor are we equipped enough to be effective. That is why God has put us in this thing called a SHIFT.

The definition of shift (verb) is to move or cause to move from one place to another, especially over a small distance.

1

You must understand that going through a shift, most of the time makes the process seem so long. We might have word spoken over our lives that sounds great to the ear, but the thing is God time is not our time. A lot of the time we don't like shifts because it causes us to go in a different direction from what we had planned. It moves us in a slight change of position. It is hard, and I do mean hard for us to embrace the first shift that God allows us to go through.

Why is it so hard you may ask? Well, have you ever been at a place in your life when everything is going great? Nice car, great job, loving relationship. It seems like you're on top of the world. Then suddenly you start losing one thing after another.

I experienced this very thing in 2007 while working at Allied Waste Services in San Carlos, Ca. at the time I was on top of the world working in my career in the waste industry. I had just gotten my third promotion in 2 years; I was making $81,000 per year. Had just purchased a 2007 Chevy Avalanche and was preparing a down payment for my first house. I was Pastoring a rapidly growing church and getting ready to take over another ministry in a neighboring city. All of a sudden there was a note given to me at work, notifying me of a lay off that included me. Because of this lay off I couldn't afford my new Avalanche and had to turn it in to the dealership. And at the same time the building that housed the new ministry was snatched from under us. This all in just a 6-month span.

This was a major test of my faith, because I was trusting God with everything, he had given me and now it had seemingly vanished. However, There is no better example of how quickly things can fall apart then the story of Job. He lost everything, only to find out that losing everything was just the process to a greater blessing. Sometimes in ministry, we could have everything together, preaching and teaching the word of God with revelation & conviction. People are tithing faithfully; the power of God is moving, and It seems as if the seats are filling up. Then all at once things come to a halt. Although you haven't lost anything at this point it feels like you have and that feeling causes you to feel empty.

It's at this point we start searching for a reason why, instead of embracing where you are and going through the process. In fact, your answer to why is simply that God has caused you to be put in this shift, it's called PROCESS.

Process is a series of actions or steps taken in order to achieve a particular end.

Thus, says the Lord of hosts, the God of Israel to all who were carried away captive, whom I have caused to be carried away from Jerusalem to Babylon. (Jeremiah 29:4 NKJV)

We never want to think that God will cause us to get in a position where we are in a very vulnerable place in our lives. When you read Jeremiah chapter 29 you find that it was God who caused them to be carried out from their homeland into Babylon. Can you imagine the one person that you trust more than anything causing you to be overtaken by your enemy, circumstances, health issues, family issue, lack of finances or whatever other situation you might encounter? It can definitely leave you in a place of uncertainty and a state of total confusion.

For another example, we could look back at the Story of Job. The bible tells us that there was a conversation between God and Satan that went in part like this:

and the Lord said to Satan, "From where do you come? So, Satan answered the Lord and said, from going to and fro on the earth and from walking back and forth on it. Then the Lord said to Satan. "Have you considered my servant Job, that there is none like him on the earth, a blameless and upright man, one who fears God and shuns evil". (Job 1:7-8 NKJV)

In order to get Job to a great blessing, God caused him to be in a very vulnerable place. For instance, he literally lost everything important to him. He lost his children, his business and it put a serious strain on his marriage. With having lost everything near and dear to him, this could have very easily put him in a depressive state and caused him to literally give up.

Not only Job though, in the book of Acts, it talks about the

Damascus experience between Jesus and Saul which caused Saul to lose his sight. After regaining his sight Saul was transformed into Paul and was given a thorn or an issue to deal with in order to keep him humbled in the process of getting him to where he needed to be in the Kingdom. This process was necessary for Saul to be effective as The Apostle Paul.

Even as a new Christian there is a process you must go through just like when you are born into this world. Everyone is so excited about the new baby. However, there was a 9-month process that you had to go through before birth. You must develop and grow in the womb. Your legs, arms, head, heart, lungs and other key parts of the body need time to grow. A baby born 25 weeks or earlier has a less chance of survival then a child born at 27 weeks. When you are not birth right or come too early, it can cause your purpose to die before it has had a chance to live. After birth, there is yet another process but a different one that you must go through, and it allows you to mature. We learn to move, crawl, walk and talk. We start learning behaviors by watching the people around us. All these things take time to develop. The only thing you know to do from the time you are born until the time you die is how to cry. As we move through our childhood up through our teen years, it causes us to go through the process of finding out who we are. It tells you that you are either a leader or a follower. It also lets us know if we are willing to work hard in school or just be average. If this growth process is true in life, then why do we think that as soon as we get saved that you should be put in a position in ministry. We think just because you can preach you should start pastoring or that you know more than the pastor. You could be the best singer in the church, but it doesn't make you the perfect choice for the praise and worship leader. You must follow the process. There is no way you can be a leader of anything if you don't first know how to follow or how to go through process.

I'm sure you're very proud of your education and the degrees that you may have but it doesn't automatically guarantee that you're qualified to lead a church. One thing that is guaranteed though is that we all must go through process at some point and as I said earlier process is not easy at all. It puts you in a place where you don't know which way to go. It will leave you searching for answers that you can't seem to find. Process will have you wondering why and for how long? But I can testify this, if God has allowed you to go through the process, it is taking you through to get you to "greater" Not to harm you.

TWO

ADAPTING TO THE SHIFT

I'M ORIGINALLY FROM ARKANSAS AND I was raised in a small town called Goodwin. I'm used to dirt roads, Grassy fields, and farm animals all around my house. Where I'm from you can tell the seasons by how it feels outside. The weather always gave you a sense of what time of year it was. I can remember driving down the road behind a tractor causing the slowest traffic I've ever driven in. Well then, I moved to California and suddenly everything I was used to was now a thing of the past. Everything that seemed so simple was hard, so I immediately had to adapt to slow traffic all the time and no dirt roads but lots of crossing freeways and highways with potholes. The weather was extreme; it changed as the day went along. In the morning it was cold, by noon it would be warm then not long after sunset it would be cold all over again. I had to learn to adapt to my surroundings. In the process of adapting I made sure I had a jacket in the car for when the weather changed, and I had to have the patience to drive in crazy slow traffic.

So, why adapt you may ask? Why not just go back to what I knew, and what was easy? Well, I found a better job here in California then I had in Arkansas, so in order to keep that job, I had to adapt to things in the bay area.

I worked 15 minutes from home, my children's school was right down the street and there was a lot of nice places to eat and shop.

It was a good change for me. We must understand that not all adjustments that you have to make will be bad.

When you are in Christ you have to learn to adjust. When you ask God for a greater anointing you must know something has to adjust. There is more praying and fasting. There is more studying. You are trying to make sure that you are on point. As you are navigating through your Christian walk the way you talk should be different. The way you act should be different and the way you react to things should be different. When all the right adjustments are made it gives you a sense of accomplishment. It gives you a feeling like you got it together. You feel like you are right there with the word when it says,

to whom much is given, from him much will be required and to whom much has been committed, of him they will ask the more. (Luke 12:48 NKJV)

Now you have it and everything is looking up for you. However, that is not all to the story. After being in East Palo Alto, California for a few years; after finding a good job 15 minutes from home, I moved to a city call Los Banos. This place was so familiar because even though it was California it looked and felt like I was back in Arkansas. The only thing about this familiar place it was no longer 15 minutes from work but 1 hour and 45 minutes from work and that was without traffic. So, there was a huge adjustment in this move. I now had to get up hours earlier then I had been, and I had to prepare for the day different from what I had gotten used to doing. There was even more traffic to deal with. Even though I lived in a less desirable place; Even though I didn't like the place I was living, a lot of people were moving there. Why were they moving there you may ask? Because we like being in places that don't give us challenges. A lot of times we have a desire to deal in familiar places. Not that the places are good for you. Most times we hang in familiar places because it reminds us of a simpler time in life. Times when we're not being uncomfortable, times when we didn't have to fight as much for the things we wanted or times when we didn't have to pray so hard or dig in the word as much.

Even times when we we've been riding on another person's faith. It takes us to a time when everything felt good. Being in places like this, only stunt your growth. We love it when things are on easy street. How many of us have made the statement "I wish I can go back to the time I didn't have any bills". The other one is "I wish I could be back in the house with mom and dad". Let's be very honest here. If we would have stay at home with mom and dad or went back to the time that we had no bills. Where would we be at right now.

A lot of things that we learned by being on our own has made us stronger and wiser. There are things that happened to you that made you call on the name of Jesus. Being on our own increased our prayer life. It made you dig trying to find a word for your situation. Every time you called on God, He came to our recuse. Yes, it cost you some sleepless nights. Nights that only you and God knew about; however, it is through these times that you found a great relationship with God.

When you're going through the shift you must adapt to where you are. You may have to start doing things different because what was working before is not working in this place of shift. You may need to get up a little earlier to pray. You may have to spend more time with God. You may have to study his word even more. You must recognize where you are and adjust. The place you're in is not a desirable place but you find that not just you are in this place at this time. Although it feels like it, you are not alone. We all go through a season of shift when we must do more because of where we are in the shift.

The best thing about all of this is that after my time there and then moving from Los Banos, I can now tell people on their way to live there what to look out for. I can tell them where to go but most importantly I can tell them how to go in and out of the city. If you don't know how to maneuver around the city that you never been in without GPS, you are bound to be lost. In a place of shift you must always keep your spiritual GPS on. If it's not working, God will always send you someone that have been there to help lead you in and out the city called Shift.

Paul said it like this when writing a letter to the people in Philippi

not that I speak of want: for I have learned, in whatsoever state I am, there with to be content. (Philippians 4:11 KJV)

The word content speaks to when you are in a state of peace. You must find peace in this because without peace during this time you will feel like you're losing your mind. You must make up your mind that you will walk in peace and not in anger. Being angry about where you are will not help at all. It only leads to crying and complaining. Allow God to humble you so you can understand the shift you are in. The Word of God tells us to,

Humble yourselves therefore under the mighty hand of God, that he may exalt you in due time. (1 Peter 5:6 KJV)

The more you humble yourself, the faster you will adapt to the shift. The hand of god is always there. Even though you will need to adapt in your shift don't get comfortable. A shift is not made for you to remain there. It is only there to get you from where you are to where you need to be. You should only adapt with the understanding that you are not going to stay in this place long. To many times we go through a shift in life or in our spiritual walk and because we do not know how to adapt, then that shift becomes a home for us

THREE

THE MIND SHIFT

BEING PHYSICALLY PREPARED AS AN athlete is very important to compete in any sport. You must work out and train hard in order to have the body strength and skill set that will help make you a great player. Honestly though that is only 50% of what it takes to becoming a great athlete. The other 50% is mental. You must have the ability to think. Which means your mind has to be worked out and worked on as well.

In the 1997 NBA Finals, it was the Chicago Bulls vs The Utah Jazz. Michael Jordan went into the game with the flu. The series was tied 2-2. Jordan had to play or risk going down 3-2 to the Jazz. It all started out shaky but in the 2nd quarter Jordan scored 17 points. The Bulls won the game 90-88 but with Michael Jordan that night scoring 38 points, 7 rebounds, 5 assists, 3 steals and 1 block. With every timeout taken, it was like you could see him talking to himself to get his body to agree with his mind. You could see him telling himself "I can do This".

If we were in church, we would say,

"I can do all things through Christ who strengthens me". (Philippians 4:13 NKJV)

But on this specific night in a Stadium The strength of God propelled Michael Jordan's mind to overcome the Flu.

You as a Man or Woman of God may not want to admit that

there are times when ministry, being a Pastor or leader in church has taken a toll on your physical bodies. Then when you hit the shift it starts playing tricks on your mind. Now we are sitting trying to figure out what happened because the devil has hit us with spiritual Flu like symptoms.

According to scripture the bible proclaims:

Therefore, if any man be in Christ, he is a new creature. Old things are passed away. Behold, all things are become new. (2 Corinthians 5:17 KJV)

That tells me that I have an opportunity to be new every day. Every day when I go before the Lord in his presence, he gives me another chance to get it right. However, I can't remain the same person I was the day before. We should want to change and that starts with the mind. The bible also clearly states that:

The steadfast love of the Lord never ceases; his mercies never come to an end; They are new every morning; great is your faithfulness. (Lamentations 3:22-23 ESV)

So, God is willing to give us a new start if we are willing to change. The only way you can change is by changing your mind. Our minds must be renewed every day. Regardless of how we feel physically. There should be a greater maturity of the mind every day.

You must be willing during the shifting season of your life, to do what the Word tells us to do:

Casting down imaginations and every high thing that exalt itself against the knowledge of God. And bringing into captivity every thought to the obedience of Christ. (2 Corinthians 10:5 KJV)

You must smash warped thinking and throw out every ungodly image that the devil has put in your mind. If you don't throw them out, you will be looking at things that are really a mirage to make things appear worse than what they really are.

Disregard anything that makes you feel that God is punishing you. Get rid of anything that tells you or makes you think that God somehow has diminished his love for you. You must bring those thoughts into captivity. You must learn how to control your thoughts, or your thoughts will control you. When we allow our thoughts to control us, our emotions put us in a state of self-pity.

The reason I know is because I have lived in that state. A place where I felt nothing was going to work out for me. I felt like God had left me and no one else cared. I was in that state of mind until I realized that I was in a shift and that God still had purpose for me. It was in that moment of realization that I was able to change my mind set.

I had been allowing my body and my willingness to do God's will be weakened because I was spiritually hit with flu like symptoms. I started to physically feel tired in my body. When I got home from work, I was so drained that I wasn't wanting to do anything and wasn't even spending time with God. I had cut my prayer time significantly and my love for studying the word of God was almost nonexistent.

One day I was scrolling through Facebook and came across a video of a church singing "Ain't no harm in keeping your mind stayed on Jesus". As I listened what continued to *come to my mind was:*

But his delight is in the law of the Lord and in His law, he meditates day and night. He shall be like a tree planted by the rivers of waters. That brings forth it's fruit in its season, whose leaf also shall not wither, and whatever he does shall prosper. (Psalms 1:2-3 NKJV)

I began to change my mindset. I told my body that it had to come into agreement with my mind. I choose to prosper not wither. I chose to live and not die. As a Pastor, a Prophet and a leader, people were depending on me to be at my best even though I was a little weak. I had to put my emotions in check; a lot of your emotions can cause you to speak and do the wrong things and be out of order.

As I started to meditate on God's word it put me in a place of peace. When my peace came, my joy came back. I understood then that where I was, was in a place of mental training. I was in training for the next season, next assignment, and next level of anointing in my life.

Just as I did, you have got to get to a place where your mind is saying "no matter what" I will push my way through. Especially in those times when it seems as if the devil won't loose his hold on you, you have to take it to another level. Find yourself doing what has be proven to work for years:

But this kind does not go out except by prayer and fasting. (Matthew 17:21 NASD)

You must get in a place where You are praying even more. Not just praying but praying with the right posture. It will also cause us to turn down our plate and consecrate ourselves by getting in the presences of God. That way you can hear from God and get a breakthrough. During this process the time will come when you need to turn off the TV, maybe get off of Facebook, Instagram & Twitter for a little while so that you can truly get into the face of God. I can guarantee that you will get God results.

The word stop cannot be in your vocabulary unless you are telling the devil what he has to stop doing in your life. Even though you are going through a shift, it is important that you keep working. When you are up for a promotion at your job and you interview for the position, you cannot go back to your desk and say I am not going to do my job until they decide whether or not they are going to hire me for this promotion. You would cause yourself to get fired. Now you're without a promotion and a without job. If this is not how it works in the natural world, what makes you think it's going to work in God's Kingdom?

When you are going through a shift you can't afford to stop working on the vision. If you stop, who will push the vision? You know that Jesus was famous for saying:

I must work the works of him that sent me, while it is day; the night cometh, when no man can work. (John 9:4 KJV)

While you are alive, you should find yourself doing God's will. When you die you can't work, and if you stop working during a shifting point in your life, then your time is wasted. The one thing I learned about being an athlete is that, just because the score is not in your favor, doesn't mean you can take plays off. You will never catch up that way. In the kingdom you can't pick and choose what day you're going to do God's work and when you're not.

When you're in a shift you must work hard just to remind yourself that it won't be like this always. God is taking me to a Greater Place!

FOUR

OVERCOMING HINDERANCES & DISTRACTIONS

As YOU READ THE WORD of God to get an understanding of what God is saying to you, the devil is thinking of ways to stop you from getting to the place in God where you need to be. It's our desire to please God. It is the Devil's job to block you. There are two devices that the devil uses a lot which are hindrances and distractions. He uses these devices and tactics to impede our focus and work. When you are focused on your vision you can be so in tune with what you are doing that you don't see the plot of the enemy. A hindrance is a person or thing that makes a situation difficult or the act of making it difficult for someone to act or for something to be done. A distraction is something that makes it difficult to think or pay attention or something that amuses or entertains you so that you do not think about problems, work, etc. Even though they do the same thing in making things difficult, they are two different challenging events. The Scripture says:

Ye Did Run well; who did hinder you in that ye Should not obey the truth? (Galatians 5:7 KJV)

One of the things about a hindrance is, trying to figure out who hindered you. Was it someone close to you? Was it someone that hates the very sight of you or was it simply you! How can a

15

person hinder you? Great question: One way is when people don't understand God's will for your life, they tend to fight against you to try and stop what you are doing. You can find a great example of this in the Word of God with, whom else but Jesus himself. According to John the fifth chapter, it tells us that Jesus healed the man at Bethesda. Remember the awesome words that he spoke to the man at the pool when Jesus said,

Rise take up your bed and walk. (John 5:8 KJV)

What a great and amazing miracle that took place. However, the leaders of the Jews were very upset because he did the miracle on the Sabbath. Then a few verses down it says,

"For this reason, the Jews (The people he loved it and was sent to) persecuted Jesus and sought to kill him. (John 5:16 KJV)

I believe that it wasn't because he did the miracle on a Sabbath. I really believe that they didn't understand his mission nor his vision. Why would I say that, it's because they were people who we would call traditionalist? They are people that don't like change. They are advocates of maintaining tradition, especially when it comes to change, so much so that they resist change and will do everything in their power to stop change from happening. As the world progressively change around us, God sends men and women in the church that have progressive minds and vision. Even though your vision will not make the word of God weak nor cause the message of God to diminish, Traditionalist won't be able to understand it; they'll say, "We've been doing it like this for 30 years". Even though the way they've been doing it stopped working 20 years ago.

Then we have the people that are working as agents for the devil and don't know it. They are doing the Devil's dirty work, but they think they are doing things for the right reasons. The Bible clearly states:

For we wrestle not against flesh and blood, but against principalities, against powers, against the rulers of the darkness of this world, against spiritual wickedness in high places. (Ephesians 6:12 KJV)

I challenge you to stop putting your focus on straightening out the person that you consider your enemy, but rather focus more on who is controlling the person. It is significant that you recognize whom you are fighting against. You are in a spiritual war fare. You are fighting against witches and warlocks, against people that don't even know that they are demon possessed. For this reason, you should always be very vigilant and on your toes. You should use your spiritual weapons to fight against the devil. The Bible says:

for the weapons of our warfare are not carnal, but mighty through God to the pulling down of stronger holds. (2 Corinthians 10:4 KJV)

So, you must use faith, read the word of God, praise and worship as your weapons. You have to pull down every stronghold.

You have the power to cast of the devil out by using our weapons that is why he wants you to doubt, stop praying, stop reading God's word, stop praising God and stop having your intimate time with God. If the enemy can stop all of that then he can stop your Assignment, your mission, your vision or simply kill your anointing.

Now there is one hindrance that comes, and it takes us by surprise. You really never see it coming. As a matter of fact, it is with you all the time. This hindrance is called self-hindrance or self-sabotage. That is right, a lot of times You hinder yourselves. You talk yourself right out of a blessing, right out of your healing, right out of deliverance and into a place of being stagnancy. Just because it doesn't look the way God showed you doesn't mean you have to stop. I've learned through life experiences how not to see things through my own eyes but to look at them through God's eyes". You have to ask God to show us the way he sees it. When you get frustrated, when things are not looking right or because the shifting process is taking longer than you feel like it should take. Seems like everyone else is getting blessed and you are not. Then you allow your words and bad decisions to stop you right in your tracks. **The Bible warns you,** *thou art snared with the words of thy mouth. (Proverbs 6:2 KJV)*

In another version it says:

then you are trapped by your own words. (Proverbs 6:2 CEV)

That means that when you speak against your own self, then you are bound by your own words. However, if you learn how to decree the right words, you can see different results.

thou shalt Also Decree a thing, and it shall be established unto thee; and the light shall shine upon his way. (Job 22:28 KJV)

Now that was a good place to shout GLORY!! While you are going through a shift keep speaking over what God has given you. Keep decreeing the words of the Lord. Keep standing on God's word; keep giving him glory, keep giving him praise. The shift is not to kill you, but it is to build you. So, at the end of the shift you know it's going to be all right.

In the game of football there are some places that are simple plays. It allows the offense and defense to focus on their jobs without adjustments. However, if the quarterback is beating the defense with the offense, the defense will try and confuse the quarterback by disguising their defense. They do this by moving the defensive line from side to side. Moving the linebackers up to the line of scrimmage and back into coverage; all of this is to distract the quarterback from doing his job. In life there can be many distractions. Whether it's on your job, in your personal life or if it's in your spiritual life. Distractions are there to do one job and that is slow you down by moving your focus from one place to another. While I was writing this book and being focused on this chapter, I got so distracted that I started to end the book. The thing about a distraction, is you can be looking at it right in the face and never consider that what you were looking at is a distraction. Most distractions are an inside job. It comes from people, places, and things that are close to you. I have found out that most distractions start small, just to catch your eye and before you know it you are out of focus with your assignment. Problems at home are one of the most common distractions the devil uses for the ones that are family oriented. Our loved ones can become a big distraction. There are many statements that we could rely on when it comes to family stability but the one that rings most true is that prayer has to be in the forefront because praying together is very important when it comes to keeping distractions from your home. The devil doesn't care who he uses. The best way to keep him out of your home is to pray together. When you are into it with your mate or the children aren't acting right, it can often times cause you to switch your focus from your assignment.

The workplace is another distraction that connects to our focus. I don't know about you but while I am at work God would drop a little nugget of revelation on me. At lunch I can be Praying, and God will begin to speak clearly to me then suddenly an issue at work can mess your whole day up. The worst part of work distraction is that you don't know how to leave it at work. Essentially you take it home and now you have more problems at home because you took out your work issues on your families. This ultimately causes more distraction.

Now let's talk about church distractions. Oh yes, there are many of them. You might actually be shocked to find out just how many distractions are in the church. And why you might ask why is there so many? Well, think about it where is the best place to slow down your progress? The easiest place for the devil to get busy is in the church. The first thing that he does is divide us with power struggles. The Pastor can't be the pastor because the deacon wants to tell the pastor what to do or not to do. You may have the member that knows everything and nobody else can do anything right. You also have a person in the choir that feels as if they should lead all the songs and tends to get very upset if they don't get to lead at least one song every Sunday. But that's not where it stops, you also have the member that always has something to say about what the church is doing with the money; however, they never give any money to the church. Then you have the church folks that are always late or come once or twice a month but they're always the first ones asking for prayer. All these things can be a distraction. The first thing to do to fight this kind of distraction is to pray. The Bible says,

Man ought always to pray and not to faint. (Luke 18:1KJV)

Men and women of God, if we are in constant contact with God, he will not let anything slip up on you. The next thing we must fight

The Devil with is the instruction God has given us about our leaders. The Word of God comm*ands us to:*

Obey them that have the rule over you and submit yourselves: For they watch for your souls, as that they must give account, that they may do it with joy, and not with grief: for that is unprofitable for you. (Hebrews 13:17 KJV)

If you obey this simple rule, then our churches will be more productive. It is not good when you grieve the man or woman of God. When the church is in order then the body can function right. If the leader of the church has a spiritual headache then it causes the body not to the movies. If there is anything you want to do, it should be to take pressure off of your Leaders. Once you get rid of the distractions in the church then people can get saved, delivered and set free. It will also cause your church to grow.

FIVE

STAYING OBEDIENT IN THE SHIFT

LET'S BE HONEST HERE. ONE of the hardest things to do is to stay focus on your assignment when chaos breaks loose in your life. When your mind and thoughts are all over the place and your emotions have failed you. During those times is when you could get your best results, as long as you stay obedient to your assignment. The Craziest thing to me is that God most times waits until you are going through changes yourself, to have people call you for help in the very times you need to help yourself. I can remember having issues in my life that had not been resolved. It seems like everyone that I spoke to need it to help in the same area. I was in a state of mind that I didn't want to help anyone. Every time I would say that I was tired and didn't want to help anyone, God would simply say, "obey your assignment". The Bible tells us without being apologetic that we should,

Preach the word; be instant in season, out of season reprove, rebuke, exhort with all long-suffering and doctrine. (2 Timothy 4:2 KJV)

In other words, there are no offseason. When God called you, he knew that there was going to be a time when being obedient to your assignment was going to be hard. He knew that at some point you would question if you could do the job or not. It is at that moment that God will remind you of what Paul said,

I am convinced and confident of this very thing, that he who has begun a good work in you will [Continue to] Perfect and complete it until the day of Christ Jesus [The time of his return]. (Philippians 1:6 AMP)

What God is actually doing during this time is allowing you to help yourself while you are helping others while they are going through their situation.

Sometimes in ministry it can become a very lonely journey. It is easy to find yourself in the middle of hundreds of people but yet find yourself all alone. Even though people are talking to you and touching you and depending on you, it feels like you are standing by yourself. To be totally honest my friends, church can be a very cold place. People love you one day and don't know you the next. People will support you one day then denounce you the very next day. It is in these times that God wants you to get closer to him. See, sometimes we get so busy working the vision and trying to figure everything out that we lose focus and can't hear God. We stop praying and studying. We get consumed with the members business and it causes us to get caught in the middle of stuff.

I asked one pastor why they spent so much time in the house and their response was, "if I stay in the house and pray I never have to worry about people saying I was in their business or them seeing me doing anything out of the will of God".

In staying obedient we have to sometimes lose. We have to give up some things that we like that is not necessarily a sin, it just may be something that hinders you from being totally obedient. There may be places you go or people you are around. It can just be how you do a certain thing.

Wherefore seeing we also are compassed about with so great a cloud of witnesses, let us lay aside every weight, and sin which doth So easily be set us, and let us run with patience the race that is set before us. (Hebrews 12:1 KJV)

The word weight means; a body's relative mass or the quantity of matter contained by it, giving Rise to a downward force; the heaviness of a person or thing. So, anything or person that has you going in a downward spiral is considered a weight to you. It can be a person at work, at church, in the community, a friend or even in your family. Sadly, you have to sometimes cut some stuff loose in order to stop sinking from all the weight. I remember a time when I was struck with a decision whether to continue the way I was going or stop. The thing was, I wasn't doing anything that we would consider sin. I love playing video games, at the time it was a stress release for me. For years, anytime I needed to release from stress I would play a video game for hours on end. I started noticing that During the times that were my regular study and prayer hours I would find myself playing video games. It wasn't clear to me what was going on at the time, until I noticed myself not praying or reading the Bible like I had been. Sometimes I would miss two or three days a week then I noticed that things in my life we're getting off-balance. After a while everything started spinning out of control. As I tried to figure out why my life was on a downward spiral, I continued to play the video games. Then one day, the voice of the Lord spoke to me and said, "You have made this video game your god". Immediately, I stopped and repented.

There were times when I would hear God say things to me, he would give me the revelation of his word and I would miss it because I was into the game. The video game itself was not sin; however, it created weight in my life. So, I had to remove it from my life. Anything that can take you away from your time with God is not worth it.

We all know what sin is. But, in the Google dictionary sin is defined as an immoral act considered to be a transgression against divine law. Christian Hamartiology describes sin as an act of offense against God. That tells us that any act that is offensive to God is sin. Anything that takes you in the opposite direction of God is sin. Once you have entered into sin it brings about a separation between you and God. It shows your weakness and it shows your lack of self-control. When we allow sin to continue it shows our inability to recognize the tricks and traps of the enemy. When we are focused on doing the will of the Lord, the enemy uses tricks and traps to catch us up in sin.

One of the easiest ways to get into sin is also one of the hardest ways to get out. That is by tricking you into falling into a sin that you enjoy doing. When you start into it you are confident that the first time doing this would also be your last time, however now you are in so deep that your life is off balanced. It also doesn't help when the people that are there to cover you in the spirit are also covering up your sin. There is no way that people can cover you in the spirit if they agree with you in your sins. You should always have someone around you that has enough God in them to tell you when you are wrong!!!

Satan will cause a delay in your shift. It can blind you to what the enemy is doing to you. You think everything is fine, but the devil is stealing your anointing. Then you will be like Sampson and you will shake yourself and can't feel any power. All you need to do is repent to God and mean it. Do the same thing that David did when he said,

create in me a clean heart, O God, and renew a steadfast (Right) spirit within me". Do not cast me away from your presence, and do not take your Holy Spirit from me. Restore to me the joy of your salvation and uphold me by your generous spirit. (Psalms 52:10-12 KJV)

You can always turn back to God. It is never too late to turn back to him. He is always waiting on you. You are the only one that God wants to use to fulfill his purpose in you.

The key to all of this is to understand that this race is a long-distance race. It is not a 100-yard dash. You have to have patience. The Bible tells us,

I have seen something else under the sun: the race is not to the swift for the battle to the strong, nor does Food come to the wise or wealth to

the Brilliant or favor to the Learned; But time and chance happen to have them all. (Ecclesiastes 9:11 NIV)

I want to assure you of something, God wants to use you and if you stay obedient, he will do just that. Everything that has been spoken over your life will manifest through your obedience.

SIX

IT MATTERS HOW YOU GO THROUGH THE SHIFT

WE ALL GO THROUGH CHANGES in life. Some are good for us and some are bad for us. Either way we see the changes, it matters how you go through them. A lot of the changes that we go through don't always start off so good in our eyes. In a shift you go through many emotions. Some days you are upbeat and on top of the world, other days you are having a battle within yourself because you are trying to figure things out. Then comes those days that you don't want to be bothered at all; You don't want to talk to anybody, you don't want to be around anybody, and you don't want to even be around yourself. However, since you can't separate yourself from yourself you just have to deal with yourself. I know it sounds awful, but it happens. Your enemies can cause you to stay in your shift longer then you want to or have to. Emotions can cause you to look at things in a way that will take things out of reality into an idealistic or notional idea. They will allow you to see only what you want to see and not the reality of what you need to see.

I was at a Denny's talking to a group of people as we conversed that day the prophetess looked at me and said, "this Year you will go through a lot of changes. It will be good for you though." Needless to say, when the changes began, my whole world was rocked. It got to the point where I felt like I had lost everything. The thing about some shifts is that, God plays the isolation game. He will isolate you from everybody that you depend on for help when you go through. It seems as if no one calls or texts you to see how you are doing and God hasn't sent anyone with a word for you. It's because he needs some time with you by himself. When there is a great call on your life it causes for a great shift. God is preparing you for greatness. That is why you must remember what God said to you in His word.

"*I will never leave nor for sake you. (Hebrews 13:5 KJV)*

"*Be strong and courageous. Do not be afraid or Terrified because of them, for the Lord your God goes with you; he will never leave you nor for sake you*". (Deuteronomy 31:6NIV)

That is why it is so important to have the mind of Christ. The Bible tells us emphatically "*Let this mind be in you which was also in Christ Jesus. (Philippians 2:5 KJV)* He went through the ultimate shift when he went to the cross for our sins.

A lot of times we quote scripture because it sounds good. During a shift: Scriptures will be tested. One of the favorite scriptures we love to quote is where it says, "*I will bless the Lord at all times; his praise shall continually be in my mouth.*" (Psalms 34:1 NKJV) That very saying will be tested during the shift. Why, you may be wondering? Because, if the devil can take away your praise, he can delay your blessing. The devil knows that if your hands can stay up you will have the victory. And going through the middle of the shift your praise is important. Why praise God you may ask, when you praise God when you are going through it is a good indication that you are on your way out. It tells the devil; you have hit me with your Best punch, but I am still dancing. Just like Moses in Exodus, as long as his hands stayed up Israel won. When his arms got heavy and dropped, they started losing. At times when your arms get heavy or your legs get tired of praising ask God to send you someone to help lift your arms or even dance for you. When you praise God with all your might, while you're going through, it confuses the enemy. Just when he thought you were down for the count. Your praise helps you bounce back. I wonder if anybody has a bounce back praise in your spirit. I know that this is very cliché, however in the mist of the shift you have to be able to praise your way through.

I have to admit, it took more than just my praise to get me through. There were times when no sound would even come out of my mouth. The only thing I could do was cry. With tears running down both sides of my face and there was no human man or woman to really talk to about the business of my pain. All I knew how to do was go into worship. All I could do was call on the name of Jesus. When you are in a shift, you must have some worship time with God. God desires to have a deeper more intimate relationship with you. In the times when there are no words God just wants to be there to rock you and allow you to find your hiding place in him. According to scripture, David said

"you are my hiding place you shall preserve me from trouble's; you shall surround me with songs of deliverance." (Psalms 32:7 NKJV) when it seems as if your praise won't come God will hide you and sing songs of deliverance to you. You have to get delivered out of that place where your mind is telling you that you are not going to make it. Get delivered from that place when your mind is telling you that there is no end in sight. You have to get out of that place that makes you want to give up. I know I can get some witnesses that will say that late in the midnight hour when no one else is around, God will come and visit you and turn your midnight into day. The more you have intimate time with God, The more you will begin to experience the Joy of the Lord. I can tell you firsthand that the joy of the Lord is your strength. There is simply nothing like it when you feel weak in your flesh, the joy of the Lord will lift you up.

I want to give you some wisdom on a personal note. I know we have people that we enjoy talking to while we are going through. It could be a friend a brother, a sister mom or dad. However, maybe it is not always good to let certain people know that you're going through. People will pretend to be your friend. They will act as if they really care for you. All the while they're just waiting to see you go through something. They will look you in the face and say to you, "I am really praying for you", however they are actually happy that you are going through. You have to allow God to send you someone that you can confide in. That one person should be strong enough and anointed enough to help pray you through. That same person should have enough God in them to see where you are and to get you passed that place. You have to ask God to send you a Jonathan. During those times I need someone that will even defy their closest friend to keep my pain a secret. They also have to have enough Holy Ghost to let you know when it is time to stop crying, get up and move forward! The person that is your Jonathan should be able to recognize who you are in the spirit. They should love you enough to tell you where the attack is coming from. Even if the attack is coming from someone they love. Once you find that Jonathan it should be a spiritual bond that bonds you two together. Everybody can't be your Jonathan. Especially, if their lips can't hold water!

SEVEN

FAITH FOR THE SHIFT

WHEN WE TALK ABOUT SHIFTING, we should always talk about faith. Not just any faith but (blind faith). Overtime I've found a personal definition of Faith and it is: Faith is what takes your thought, dreams and vision from imagination and brings it into reality. Growing up in ministry for about 20 years under Bishop Michael Thomas was the first time I saw Blind Faith exemplified when Bishop Thomas was faced with a choice. Either work one hour on Sunday before church or quit his job. I need to tell you that he had a wife and children as well. When faced with this ultimatum he did the only thing that was right to do in his eyes. He quit. Now during this shift in his life, he lost a lot of things. He never wavered in his faith. Because he went through this shift with so much faith, I have seen doors open for him year after year. I haven't seen him work another regular job since.

Some years later I met a great man of God in the person of Apostle Reginald White. I recall a time when Apostle was told he had cancer. It was him and a few of his preaching colleagues all got diagnosed at the same time. His colleagues all went through surgery and cancer treatments. I remember him telling us that he trusted God and that God was going to heal him. This was at a time in his life when Apostle had just had his apostolic affirmation. In this case promotion came first then the shift. After about a year of fasting and praying the doctors could never find the cancer in him. Although his

30

friends went through surgery they were still struggling with cancer. So, I use these two great men of faith as examples because these two men are whom I pattern my faith after.

When you begin to go through a shift you have to believe God at his word. Understanding this, that God is snared by his own word. Which means if God said it, just have faith that he will bring it to pass. Sometimes you have to walk in faith not knowing what is getting ready to happen. We all have to model this kind of faith. The faith in Exodus 14 when Moses stretched out his rod over the Red Sea and they had to wait to see if God was going to move before, they made a move. There is nothing wrong with that type of faith. Sometimes we need to see the doors opening or we need to see the vision coming together before we get excited. A lot of times we are telling God, Lord I trust you as long as you are showing me the way out. Then when we see the way being made now, we are ready to put in the work. God is now saying I need some men and women that had the faith of Joshua in the book of Joshua the 3rd chapter where God told them to stand in the Jordan before he parted the water. What God is saying to us here is that when the shift comes don't stop moving have enough faith to stand up in the middle of uncertainty and calamity while going through the shift and push forward. As soon as you see the shift coming you need to get your faith muscles to working. We know that without faith we cannot please God according to Hebrews 11:6 even in the shift you have to stay pleasing to God. Yes, you still have to do right even when you don't feel like it.

We all know that *"now faith is the substance of things hoped for, the evidence of things not seen.* (Hebrews 11:1 KJV) However, every one of us should have a personal definition of what faith is to you. I myself have one. Faith to me is trusting God to take vision from imagination to reality. When we trust God To move us from one state to the next, you have to trust him to take the vision God gave you out of your mind and bring it to reality. So, your next promotion done, your next job done, your next healing done and a great anointing or move of God in your life you can consider them all done. We are not TLC; we don't go "chasing waterfalls". We are children of the most-high God we should be chasing after God and the things of him. Through faith we shall obtain it. Everyone is not graced to go through what you are going through. They think they want your anointing. They think they want the call on your life. The question is though; do they have the faith to go through what you went through to get what you got? We should always remember as children of God that *"we walk by faith, not by sight"*. (2 Corinthians 5:7 NKJV)

According to scripture, anything that God does he always shows us the beginning and the end. He never shows you the middle on your way to your destiny. We would be trying to find a way to get around the shifts. You just have to have faith that God knows what he is doing. So, what he moved people out of your life, some will return, and some will remain gone. So, what, you lost some things. That was just God trying to give you something better. So, what, the doctor's report was not favorable. God is still a healer. You must have faith knowing that he is all those things. No matter what you go through.

At the beginning of this book I gave you the definition of faith that I grew up on. Faith is simply "for all I trust him". So just trust him. Scripture says *"trust in the Lord with all your heart and lean not on your own understanding in all your ways acknowledge him and he will direct your paths.* (Proverbs 3:5 NKJV)

All God is saying here is talk to me and allow me to put you on the right road. Even when the shift seems foggy God will not permit you to get injured while you are going through the shift. If there is any harm done, then God himself will mend you back together. I have been right where you are; trusting God while I was broken. Feeling alone while I was trusting; I assure you that if you keep the faith in Jesus Christ you will come out untouched.

How much faith do you think Shadrach, Meshach and Abednego had to have that they believed God so much so, that they were thrown in the fire? Just think of how much faith they must have had when they came out unharmed. To truly understand that the same God who allowed you to get in the fire, was the same God in the midst of the fire with you and is the same God that is going to bring you out.

Go ahead and high five yourself and say won't he do it? Now answer yourself, and say Yes, he will!!

EIGHT

THE CRUSHING DURING THE SHIFT

Now as I start this chapter, I want you to know that this is a subject that is Very important in the shift. If you really have a call on your life, then this part is going to prepare you for the next move of God in your life. During this stage that God wants to download information in your spirit. It is called the rebuilding stage. Some people call it a reboot. It allows God to take you apart and make you new and improved. We all have to go through this stage to get where we really need to be. One of the examples that we have is the crushing of the Olive. We know the best way to get the olive oil out of the olive is to crush it. Some people don't know that the olive is the fruit of the olive tree. Because of its taste you would not know that it is a fruit. Inside the Olive there is a seed called a pit. The pit of the olive is hard and sometimes it's hard to get out by the regular method. Sometimes you have to not only crush it but also dig it out. I know we want the anointing of God and we don't mind being crushed for the anointing. However sometimes it is those pits or hard things in our life that need to be dug out so we can be usable. That means God has to go beneath the surface to get out what is blocking your progress. It can be things inside of us that is in our DNA that we struggle with that can keep us from moving forward.

It could be a drinking problem, you could be a liar, you could be a cheater and the list can go on and on. These are just some things that your mother or father may have been dealing with in their DNA. Now you find that you are dealing with them and it can cause you to stumble. Somethings can be a real struggle. Even though you are saved, sanctified and filled with the Holy Spirit, you Struggle with your DNA. Low self-esteem drug addiction, depression and unruly children. If you allow God to clean you during the crush, then you will live. The Bible says *"But I came by and saw you there, helplessly kicking about in your own blood. As you lay there, I said LIVE!"* (Ezekiel 16:6 NLT)

God is saying that you don't have to stay there in your DNA and die. You can live. In the next verse it says "And I helped you to drive like a plant in the field. You grew up and became a beautiful jewel". God is going to use you to break DNA curses out of your bloodline. He is going to use you to destroy the lie that has been spoken over your life.

The next kind of crushing is the kind that comes about when God looks at you and says you are almost perfect, but he decides to change a flaw in you. There was a time where I was enjoying all the great comments and accolades that people were saying about me. I was a humble person never really said much. I was always laid back; I didn't have to always be upfront. I love the way God used me while I ministered to his people. It seemed as if everything God spoke through me never fell to the ground. Not realizing I had one flaw in my character that God was not pleased with. I was talking to a person one day and they told me; man you got this flaw in your character that will cause you to do and say things that you can't go back and fix. I know you are wondering what it is, well one thing that was a bad flaw in me is that I would react to situations first before thinking about the best way to resolve the issue. When you say and do things out of hurt and emotion, it causes you to see everything the same way. It all looks like hurt, even though you really don't have a clear picture of what is going on. A few days later that flaw showed up and God wasn't pleased. Two days after that God crushed me, he allowed me to be broken all the way down. So, I asked God why you are crushing me at this time, when you have spoken some promises over my life and things were looking up for me. He sent me to where it says *"then I went down to the potters house, and there he was, making something at the wheel. And the vessel that he made of clay was marred in the hand of the potter; so he made it again into another vessel, as it seemed good to the potter to make."* (Jeremiah 18:31-34 NKJV) The best thing about this crushing is you never leave the potters hand. Even though it will break you and it will challenge you in your face, God will never leave you broken. His hand is always upon you. Embracing this part of the shift is hard. It often times forces you to look at yourself and who you really are. What you see sometimes doesn't look like God. However, trust Him to rebuild you totally through his Holy Ghost.

Before I end this chapter, I want to talk about one more crushing that we go through that is the crushing of the cross. Scripture declares *"then Jesus told his disciples,"* if anyone will come after me, let him deny himself and take up his cross and follow me. (Matthew 16:24 KJV)

Denying yourself is one of the most selfless acts you can do. Giving up everything you like to do and everything that you can do, just to do God's will. That is an incredible act out of loyalty to God. We live in a world that at the age of 18 we believe that we are grown. We have the mindset that we can do our own thing. As the term that is so often spoken today goes "You do you and I'll do me."

When you realize that God can do you better than you can do you; It gets easier to deny yourself. When you understand that God is not trying to kill your happiness but to give you joy. Then denying yourself will take on a whole new meaning. By denying yourself you are basically getting out of your own way. God's way is always better.

Now to the cross; I have read this scripture for many years and never saw what I seen this time. As simply as it is written we still miss it. This time when I read "Take up your cross and follow me."

It made we think, the last time Jesus was carrying a cross he was on his way to be crucified!!! He wanted us to take up the very thing that was going to crush us. I then realized this is the ultimate crushing. This type of crushing is going to take you where you have never been before. This is when your own turn their backs on you. People you have helped and gave them your last. People you have prayed for. They have called you late in the midnight hour and they are on your phone crying with no words coming out of their mouth and you are listening and pouring into them, telling them that it is going to be all right. These same people you have given money to. These are people that you had their backs in their toughest times. Now they don't even know who you are. Now they don't have anything good to say about you. Everything you do now they criticize. You're not anointed enough for them. They are basically saying crucify him. Not only that but you have the battle of your own thoughts about yourself. You end up asking yourself are you good enough to lead people. Am I good enough to take this promotion? Am I good enough in this relationship? Can I build this church?

Now you feel like your reputation has been destroyed and now people don't want to hear what you have to say. It seems as if people have nailed you to the cross and they are yelling crucify him, crucify him. People don't care about the pain that you are in from the beating that life has given you. They don't care about your heart being broken. After you have helped everybody else, now you are all alone. Instead of people you have defended coming to your defense in return, those same people that you defended are now denying you. They are hiding and don't want people to know that they are connected to you. You may want to know what my answer is on this. How do you get past this you may ask? It is simple, die to it.

Die to all the hurt and pain, die to all the uncertainty, die to the people talking about you. Forgive them and then forgive yourself. Remember that Jesus didn't stay dead. As Christ was crucified, we will also be crucified. Just like Christ got up, he will resurrect us and in the same manner that Christ got up with all power we will also get up with power; the power to walk right, talk right and live right. He will resurrect us with the power to preach and teach and even with a greater anointing. Your praise will have power. Your testimony will have power behind it.

Then you will be able to say *I am crucified with Christ; nevertheless I live, yet not I, but Christ lives in me and the life which I now live in the flesh I live by faith of the son of God, who loved me, and gave himself for me.* (Galatians 2:20 KJV)

That was a great place to give God some praise!

After all this you will be able to truly say I don't look like what I have been through. You can look back at your cross and say, *O death, where is Thy sting? O grave where is Thy victory?* (1Corinthians 15:55 KJV)

You ought to let the enemy know that you have the victory!

NINE

WHAT ARE YOU SPEAKING IN THE SHIFT?

I HAVE NOTICED THAT WHEN people are upset, angry and hurt, there are many words that can enter our mind while we are thinking about the situation. It causes us at times to just open our mouth and say the first thing that will come to mind. Not realizing that as men and woman of God we must be careful of what we say. When you speak things begin to happen just because you spoke it. you don't understand that when we speak a lot of negative words, a lot of negative things will start happening in our life due to the negative things we speak out of our own mouth.

I need you to understand that no one can kill what God has spoken over your life. However, you can stop it by what you are confessing out of your own mouth.

There is a scripture in 2 Corinthians that says *"for all the promises of God in him are yes, and in him amen, to the glory of God through us.* (Corinthians 1:20 NKJV)

This means that everything God promised you. He has already said you can have it. He has already stamped his approval on it. He will make all his promises come through. Still we have to be mindful that it is the enemy's job to try and stop the promises of God from coming to us by making our confession change from God can do it, too it won't happen for me.

It is very important that you think about what you are getting ready to say before you allow the wrong thing to come out of your mouth. It can be the most dangerous form of self-sabotage and has the ability to kill your future. What we should be asking ourselves is will my words help or hurt? It is very true when people say that they are an atmosphere changer. I need to ask a question though what atmosphere are you trying to create?

If everything around you is going wrong and it seems as if your life is on a collision course with tragedy, you can change all of that by changing your confession.

We know that Proverbs says that *"death and life are in the power of the tongue: and they that love it shall eat the fruit thereof.* (Proverbs 18:21 KJV)

You can't just run your mouth because it can kill what God has made alive for you. As much as possible you need to speak the right thing. As leaders we should always be teaching people to change their confession. You also need to make sure that you are making the right confessions. Make sure that what is coming out of your mouth is not killing the vision. Make sure that what you are saying to people is blessing them and not cursing them. I recall being upset with some people a while back and I just began to speak out of anger; Words were just flowing out of my mouth. Then I realized what I did and repented to God and I asked those people to forgive me. If you are not careful you can say the wrong thing to people, and it can change their atmosphere without their permission.

The key to avoiding this is when you get angry just be quiet. The Bible has scriptures in it for a reason. The Bible clearly states

"Be ye angry and send not: let not the sun go down upon your wrath: "you need to get it straight before the next day. You don't know what may happen through the night (Ephesians 4:26 KJV)

There are a few things that you are to be confident about when it comes to God's word. The first thing is that God is faithful. God has not changed his mind about you. He still wants to use you to finish the vision. He could very easily give it to someone else however he believes in you. He has given it into your hands, that's why He's allowing you to go through what you are going through just to build you so you can finish your assignment. The next thing you need to be confident in about is when God makes a promise to us his word will not return to him void.

It says *"so shall my word be that goeth forth out of my mouth: it shall not return until me void; but it shall accomplish that which I please, and it shall prosper in the thing where to I sent it.* (Isaiah 55:11 KJV)

It absolutely must happen for you. God's words are always true. When God speaks, his word becomes alive. Hebrews says

*"For the word of God is living and powerful, and sharper than any two-edged sword, piercing even to the division of the soul and spirit, and of joints and marrow, and is a discerner of the thoughts and intents of the heart. (*Hebrews 4:12 NKJV)

So, since God's words are true then you should speak what God has already spoken. God's words have been alive and powerful from the beginning of time. Everything that He has ever spoken has been manifested. He said let there be light and so it was. So, you see, if God said it is going to be then you should get ready because it is going to be.

The last thing is that you must remember that God is not a man that shall lie!!! The scripture says

God is not a man, so he does not lie. He is not human, so he does not change his mind. Has he ever spoken and failed to act? Has he ever promised and not carried it through? (Numbers 23:19 NLT) **God cannot lie**!!!

God is going to do what he says. He will not lie to you at all and if he could lie then he wouldn't be God. It's just that simple; Therefore, since he is still God then he cannot and will not lie.

TEN

EMBRACING YOUR NEW DAY!

FOR HIS ANGER IS BUT a moment; His favor is life: Weeping may endure for a night, but joy come in the morning. (Psalms 30:5 NKJV)

"For I know the plans I have for you," says the Lord. "They are plans for good and not for disaster, to give you a future and a hope. (Jeremiah 29:11 NLT)

Behold, the days are coming; says the Lord, that I will perform that good thing which I have promised to the house of Israel and to the house of Judah: (Jeremiah 33:14 NKJV)

Let me encourage you right now that today is your new day. You have cried long enough you have suffered long enough you have been in your feelings long enough this is a new day says the Lord. Somebody open your mouth and declare "My new day is here!!"

I am so excited for you right now because after all the turmoil and havoc that broke loose in your life your ministry, on your job and in your health: Your breakthrough finally is here.

There were times when you felt like giving up, times when you wanted to walk away times when you wanted to open your mouth and speak a negative word about your shift. However, you kept pushing. You continued to believe, and you kept your focus. Now look at you; you're stronger, more powerful and more focused than ever. You're more determined to work even harder to get that promotion. You're more focused on making your family work. And it was all because you decided to walk in your shift and embrace it.

God never planned for you to come out hurt and broken. He never planned for you to come out a loser. God just had to get some stuff out of you that could derail your future. You must understand that God can see way better then we see. He already knows what our future looks like. God knows things about us that you overlooked in yourself. There are things in us that God can see that will hurt our future if they are not corrected. So God's plan all along was to get those things out of you so that you would be able to see a future and a hope.

Since you went through this shift, you are hopeful and not hopeless. You will be helpful and not helpless. You will be a blessing and not a curse. Our test has created a great testimony. Your trial has become a trophy, all because you have triumphed over and come out of the shift.

I know I know I know you thought it was the end of the world. You thought everything was over, you thought life had ended. Because of the shifts you should now have a different perspective on your life your ministry your marriage and even on your job. You can now look at other people while they are in the shift and say "just embrace where you are, it is only temporary ". You can encourage people that I made it through, and you will make it through too. And the best thing about you having made it through the shift is that you now have the tools to help them get through.

Sometimes we tend to get discouraged in the process of the shift during the waiting, but God has not forgotten what he has promised you. After all the things that you went through, he is going to perform his good works toward you. Everything that has not come to pass is getting ready to manifest. Scripture says,

"Yes indeed, it won't be long now". God's decree.

Things are going to happen so fast your head will swim, one thing fast on the heels of the other. You won't be able to keep up. Everything will be happening at once-and everywhere you look, blessings! Blessings

Like wine pouring off the mountains and hills. I'll make everything right again for my people Israel:

They'll rebuild their ruin the cities. They'll plant venues and drink good wine. They'll work their gardens and eat fresh vegetables. And I'll plant them; plant them on their own land. They'll never again be uprooted from the land I've given them." God, your God, says so. (Amos 9:13-15 MSG)

Just get ready because God is going to open the floodgates. The rain is getting ready to pour. This is the day that the Lord has made. It is the time to rejoice and be glad in this day.

When you realize that God's plan is better than any other plans, it won't be so hard to follow his plan anymore. Fighting God's plan is you fighting against your own future and destiny. God knows what he's doing; And God knows what you need. Don't lose faith in God; he has your back always.

When all is said and done, you'll be victorious so don't stop praying don't stop praising and don't stop worshiping God.

Be careful that you don't lose faith and always keep focus because your shift is just Gods way of preparing you for your next assignment your next mission and your next promotion of anointing And ultimately the next move of God in your life.

I Thank you for sharing this journey with me through "Embracing the shift" and I pray that you have been blessed.

ACKNOWLEDGMENTS

I WOULD FIRST LIKE TO thank my Lord and savior Jesus Christ for giving me the words to say. He has blessed me in so many ways. From experience, I can tell you that He will never leave you nor will he ever forsake you. Through everything I have ever been through in life God has been right there. I want to thank my mother Pastor, Dr. Helen Brown for giving birth to me. Thank you for never doubting me. When I told you that I was called to preach, you supported me when no one else did. Thank you for praying for me. You allowed me to grow and be the man of God that I am today. I would also like to thank my siblings Beverly Smith, Willie McKissick, Gerald Armstrong and Wynetta McKissick for just loving their weird little brother. I thank you Beverly Smith for being my mother figure when mom moved to California. You have been there when I really needed someone to talk to. You have played a very important part in my life. To Willie McKissick, you have always been my hero. You fought for me when I was too small to fight for myself and then you defended our country for over 20 years. If no one else thanks you, I thank you for putting your life on the line for us. Gerald Armstrong, I look up to you as a businessman. To see how you handle your business and your hard work. It makes me want to work even harder for what I want out of life. My baby sister, Wynetta McKissick, you have been with me since I started my first church. It means a lot that you always support me in ministry. To hear all the great things your co-workers, have to say about you at work makes me smile and proud that you are my sister. To Booker Smith my awesome brother in law, you keep me inspired by the revelations that God gives you. Thanks for never changing your opinion of me when others didn't understand what was going on with me. Mandy McKissick to see you grow in the Lord inspires me to be an even better Christian. To Lisa Patton thanks for your support. It is awesome to see where God has brought you to and how he has blessed you.

I want to thank my children for telling me that I could do this. You guys encouraged me so much and I love each of you with all my heart. Tashiera LeeShaye McKissick you are the planner. You always have a plan. You have so many words that are inside of you. Keep writing your songs and your books, God has greatness for you. Diominique Dayone' Marie McKissick to see you go from not doing well in high school to getting your master's degree blows my mind. To see how you are going to school, working and training up your child blesses me every day. I see your gift getting stronger and stronger. Keep using it. It will take you before great men. Waymond Dionte' McKissick, my name sake. I love you very much sir. Your music has blessed me over the years. The way you are grinding not just for yourself but for the whole family lets me know that you are going to be a great father, husband and provider one day. Keep grinding and God will make your dreams become reality. To L'Renee Rose McKissick you are the blessing of my heart. You are the last however you have carved a space out of everyone heart. You're my little beautiful princess. When the doctors said it wouldn't happen God said it could.

I want to say thank you in advance to every person that will read this book. I want to thank you for your support. I want to thank Bishop Derrick Johnson for writing my foreword. You are a brother indeed. And you have truly Blessed me over the years. To every church that has opened their doors and allowed me to come and share with them the good news of Jesus Christ, I want to say thank you. To every person that has pushed me to where I am right now, I want to say thank you. I want to thank my intercessor

Erika Echols for always keeping me lifted in prayer. To Bishop Leonard Dew for the first seed sowed into this book. To Bishop Mario Gaines, that prayed with me and talked with me when I wanted to give up. Thanks man of God. To all the men and women of God that have spoken into my life and prayed for me, thanks for your support and obeying God. To Apostle RJ White, thank you for being an awesome leader. Thank you for the things you have shared and taught me. Fresh Word Church thanks for supporting me and being there for me throughout the years with your prayers and encouragement and making me feel like I'm the best pastor in the whole world. To Greater Worship and Deliverance Church for making me feel like family and supporting me. I also want to Thank Pastor Edward and Lady Pickett along with their church New Living Word for helping me make this dream possible through prayer and financial backing. May God bless every person that has played an important part in my life.

Printed in the United States
By Bookmasters